DOCTORS IN ACTION

The PEDIATRICIAN

by
Samuel Woods

Photographs by
Gale Zucker

B L A C K B I R C H P R E S S , I N C .

W O O D B R I D G E , C O N N E C T I C U T

Published by Blackbirch Press, Inc.
260 Amity Road
Woodbridge, CT 06525

©1999 by Blackbirch Press, Inc.
First Edition

e-mail: staff@blackbirch.com
Web site: www.blackbirch.com

Printed in the United States

10 9 8 7 6 5 4 3 2 1

Special Thanks
The publisher would like to thank the administration and staff of Yale-New Haven Hospital for their valuable cooperation in putting this book together.

Library of Congress Cataloging-in-Publication Data
Woods, Samuel G.
The pediatrician / by Samuel Woods ; photographs by Gale Zucker.
     p.   cm. — (Doctors in action)
   Includes index.
   Summary: Uses the daily activities of one doctor to describe the work of a pediatrician.
   ISBN 1-56711-237-4 (lib. bdg. : alk. paper)
   1. Pediatrics—Juvenile literature. [1. Pediatrics. 2. Occupations.] I. Zucker, Gale, ill. II. Title. III. Series.
RJ78.W66 1999
618.92—dc21
                                         98-3900
                                           CIP
                                           AC

Chances are good that you have already met a pediatrician. That's because a pediatrician is a doctor that cares for kids! When you were born, a pediatrician probably gave you your first check-up in the hospital. He or she is also the doctor that treats you when you get the flu, have an upset stomach, or feel sick in other ways.

Many pediatricians work in a variety of places. Most of their hours are spent having office visits with young patients. A pediatrician may also work in a hospital, and maybe even a clinic or a shelter.

Pediatricians also help parents. They answer the many questions that new parents have about their babies. They can also help parents understand how their child is developing both emotionally and physically.

Pediatricians are special in many ways. You will see most doctors in your life only once or twice, to solve a special problem. But a pediatrician you will see over and over again for many years. Most pediatricians treat kids from the time they are born until they are age 18. Many see their patients all the way through college!

As you grow, your pediatrician will observe your progress. He or she will be there to answer your questions. Your pediatrician will know your history and will be able to advise you as you develop into an adult.

Ron Angoff has been a pediatrician for more than 20 years. Dr. Ron knew right from the start that he wanted to work with children. "Pediatricians are different from other doctors," he explains. "They have a different personality. You have to be someone who enjoys a long-term relationship with patients."

Every day, Dr. Ron sees kids of all ages. Most days, he sees healthy kids who need check-ups. These visits are called "well visits." That's because they are not for treating a problem. Instead, they are to make sure everything is okay.

Some days, Dr. Ron also sees sick kids who need special care. Sometimes the kids are in the hospital. Other times, they come to Dr. Ron's office.

Above: *Toddlers get familiar with tools.*
Below: *Weighing in*

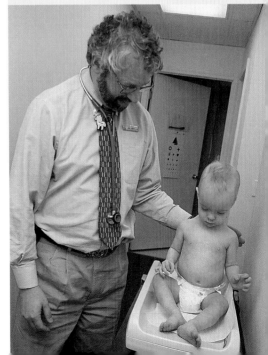

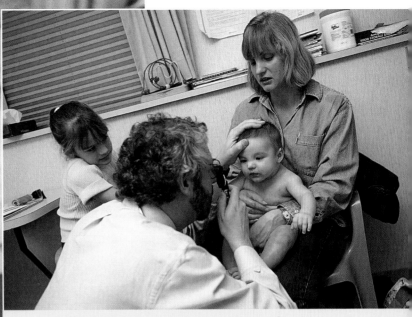

Parents always have a chance to ask questions during an examination.

Whenever he meets with his patients, Dr. Ron asks them a lot of questions. And he does a lot of listening. Because many of his patients are too young to speak, Dr. Ron also has to ask parents many questions.

"You deal with the whole family in pediatrics," Dr. Ron explains. "And you're often dealing with very young patients who are not able to tell you as much as you'd like them to."

Most doctors are very busy people. Many follow strict schedules. That's so they can organize their time properly.

What does a doctor like Dr. Ron do in an average week? Each day is a mix of different things.

On Mondays, Dr. Ron spends a lot of time meeting with other doctors. He talks about special projects and shares medical information and advice.

Early on Tuesday mornings, Dr. Ron teaches young pediatricians in the nursery of a local hospital. There, he shows other doctors how to do physical exams. He also watches them as they work with their patients.

Dr. Ron meets with hospital staff and checks X-rays (below).

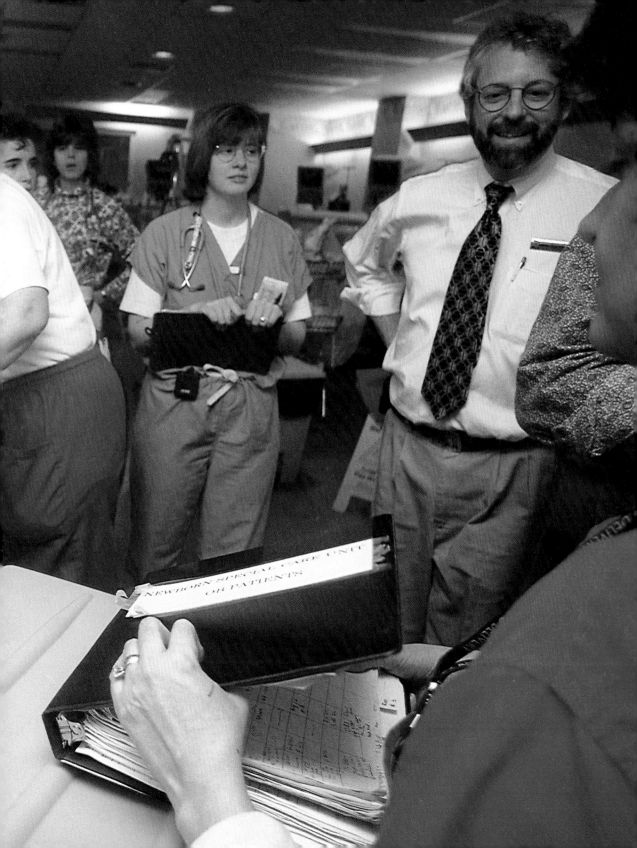

Tuesday afternoons are spent in the office. During this time, Dr. Ron does well visits with his patients.

When he does check-ups for older kids, Dr. Ron will ask them lots of questions. "How's your baby brother doing? What do you like to eat these days?" he asks one girl. He listens very carefully to the answer. He always wants to hear what his patients' lives are like.

Conversations with Dr. Ron can be about anything. "It's important for kids to feel comfortable with their pediatrician," he explains.

This is also a time for kids to tell Dr. Ron about things that may be worrying them. Some kids talk to him about nightmares. Other kids are worried about how their bodies are developing. "I don't separate the emotional issues from the physical issues," Dr. Ron says. "Talking and giving advice are part of our care."

"You hope that patients can talk to you about anything," says Dr. Ron. "This is especially true with my teen patients. They need to know they can trust me. They may have questions or fears about drugs, AIDS, or anything else."

Well visits are not just about talking. Dr. Ron must also do a physical exam. This gives him a chance to make sure everything in the body is working properly.

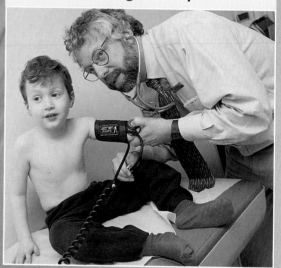

Checking the mouth and throat
Inset: Checking blood pressure

There are lots of things to check, even in a simple exam. First, Dr. Ron will look inside the ears. He makes sure that the ear canal is clear and that there is no infection. Then he'll shine a light in the eyes. This is to check that the eyes are reacting properly to brightness. After that, it's a look at the tongue and throat. Dr. Ron wants to make sure nothing is red or swollen. That would be a sign of possible illness.

Checking ears, eyes, heart, muscles, and spine are all part of an exam.

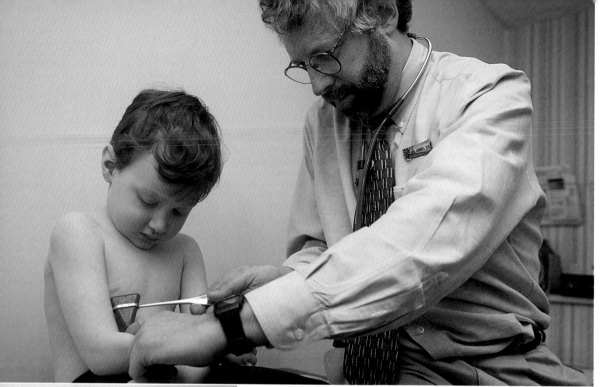

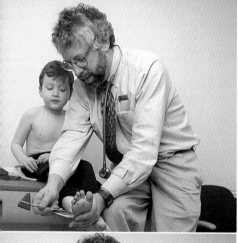

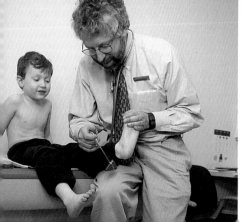

Checking reflexes is another important part of an exam. Reflexes are part of the body's nervous system. The nervous system is what your body uses to react to things.

To test reflexes, Dr. Ron uses a little rubber mallet. He taps legs and arms with the mallet in just the right places. When he does, his patients' legs or arms "jump". This shows Dr. Ron that the nervous system is working properly.

TAKING THE SHOTS

Dr. Ron says that one of the single biggest worries his young patients have is getting shots. That may be because there seem to be so many during the first 18 months of life! But worrying is usually the worst part. After getting a shot, most kids only feel uncomfortable for about a minute. Here's when the average kid gets the needle:

Birth: Hepatitis B
2 months: DTaP; Hib; OPV/IPV; Hepatitis B
4 months: DTaP; Hib; OPV/IPV
6 months: DTaP; Hib
9 months: Hepatitis B
12 months: MMR; Tuberculosis Tine Test; Varivax
15 months: DTaP; Hib; OPV/IPV
5 years: DTaP; OPV; Hgb; Tuberculosis
    Tine Test
11 years: MMR booster; Hepatitis B
15 years: DT booster

Total number of shots: 18

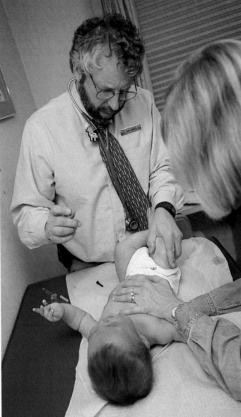

Key:

DTaP: prevents Diptheria, Tetnus , acellular Pertussis
Hib: H. influenzae type b (prevents bacterial meningitis)

OPV/IPV: vaccine to prevent polio
MMR: prevents measles, mumps, and rubella

Some more good news: Because there are so many shots—and new vaccines to prevent diseases are being developed every year—many researchers are working on ways to combine as many shots as possible. This will reduce the number of times a kid must get the needle.

Wednesday mornings are spent doing "rounds" at the hospital. This is when Dr. Ron visits sick or injured kids. It's also when he meets his newest and youngest patients: the newborns.

Dr. Ron checks on a girl who was brought to the hospital after falling down the stairs.

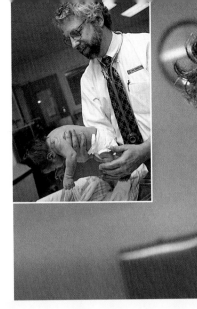

Usually within 12 hours of a birth, a pediatrician checks on a newborn. The first exam is important. It tells the doctor if the baby is strong and healthy or if there are problems. "The main thing with a newborn," Dr. Ron explains, "is to see if the baby is mature. Is it breathing ok? Is the heart ok? Is it peeing and pooping the way it should be?"

Meeting with Dr. Ron also helps parents. They can ask questions about things that worry them. The answers very often comfort them and help them to relax with their new babies.

Above: *A newborn gets an exam from a nurse.*
Below: *Dr. Ron talks with new parents.*

"One of the hardest things—one of the biggest challenges of pediatrics— is you never know what's going to walk in the door," explains Dr. Ron. "You've got to be able to recognize right away what's serious and what's not. That's a real challenge. It makes my job interesting, but also very stressful."

Five o'clock is not the end of the day for Dr. Ron. He often spends a few evening hours returning phone calls. This is also when he can arrange special care for his patients. Every fifth night and every fifth weekend Dr. Ron is "on-call." That means he is on duty for emergencies at any time of the day or night. On-call duty is shared by all the doctors in Dr. Ron's group.

During a few quiet minutes between phone calls, Dr. Ron thinks about all the young people he sees. "One of the best things about what I do is watching the kids grow up," Ron says with a smile. "And I guess the other thing is helping families work through a problem or a crisis. When we get to work through a problem together, and turn it around, that's really satisfying. That's the really rewarding stuff."

Glossary

check-up (chek·uhp) A check to see that nothing is wrong with a patient.

emergency (i·mur·juhn·see) A bad situation or injured person that needs to be handled quickly to fix.

nursery (nur·sur·ee) A place where newborn babies are first kept at a hospital to make sure they are healthy.

patients (pay·shents) Someone who is being treated by a doctor.

physical exams (fiz·uh·kuhl eg·zams) An exam that checks that everything in the body is healthy.

reflexes (ree·fleks·ez) A part of the body's nervous system used to react to things. (When a doctor tests your reflexes, he will tap your knee to see if it jumps.)

rounds (roundz) When doctors visit each of their patients in the hospital.

Further Reading

Howe, James. *The Hospital Book.* New York: William Morrow & Company, 1994.

Lee, Barbara. *Working in Health Care and Wellness* (Exploring Careers series). Minneapolis, MN: Lerner Publications Company, 1996.

Miller, Marilyn. *Behind the Scenes at the Hospital.* Chatham, NJ: Raintree/Steck-Vaughn, 1996.

Ready, Dee. *Doctors* (Community Helpers series). Danbury, CT: Children's Press, 1997.

Index